Australia's Native Trees

Above: Acorn banksia, *Banksia prionotes* (see page 26).
Left: Snow gum, *Eucalyptus pauciflora* (see page 45).

PHOTOGRAPHS BY KEN STEPNELL
TEXT BY DALYS NEWMAN

CHILD & ASSOCIATES
AN ALL-AUSTRALIAN PUBLISHER

Above: Coral tree, *Erythrina variegata* (see page 32).
Front cover: Cootamundra wattle, *Acacia baileyana* (see page 18).
Front endpaper: Wattle and river red gums on the banks of the
Murray River near Tocumwal in New South Wales.
Back endpaper: Trees of all shapes struggle for survival among
the rocks at the Mootwingee National Park in New South Wales.
Back cover: Illyarie, *Eucalyptus erythrocorys* (see page 38).

Published by Child & Associates Publishing Pty Ltd
5 Skyline Place, Frenchs Forest, NSW, Australia, 2086
Telephone (02) 975 1700, facsimile (02) 975 1711
A wholly owned Australian publishing company
This book has been edited, designed and typeset in Australia
by the Publisher
First edition 1989
Reprinted 1990
Photographs © Ken Stepnell 1989
Text © Dalys Newman 1989
Printed in Hong Kong by Everbest Printing Co. Ltd
Typesetting processed by Deblaere Typesetting Pty Ltd

National Library of Australia
Cataloguing-in-Publication data

Stepnell, Kenneth, 1931–
Australia's native trees.

  Includes index.
  ISBN 0 86777 287 5

  1. Trees—Australia. 2. Trees—Australia—Pictorial works. I.
Newman, Dalys. II. Title

635.9'77'0994

INTRODUCTION

Australia's unique trees have been a subject of fascination since first closely examined by Joseph Banks and Carl Solander when they landed with Captain Cook in 1770. They presented a strange and intriguing sight to these northern hemisphere botanists. The cold highlands lacked the extensive pine forests of the northern hemisphere and the mild temperate forests had no summer green trees that lost their leaves in winter. Instead, Australia's trees, with few exceptions, were all evergreens, often shedding their bark instead of their leaves!

Nearly 90 per cent of Australia's plants are found nowhere else in the world and to understand the uniqueness of this country's flora we must go back to 200 million years ago when Australia was part of a large land mass, known as Gondwanaland, which included South America, Africa, India, Antarctica and New Zealand. At this time much of Australia's vegetation was subtropical rainforest in a warm moist climate. About 110 million years ago, Gondwanaland began to break up until only Australia, Antarctica and South America remained together. Then, about 45 million years ago, Australia began to drift northward, eventually coming into contact with South-East Asia and plants adapted to arid, and wet tropical climates.

Climatic change and geographical isolation began to exert an increasing influence on Australian flora. The continent became drier, rainfall more erratic and long droughts were common. In places on the coast, where the rainfall remained regular and sufficient, the original moisture-loving plants survived. Elsewhere they had to adapt to the drier conditions or become extinct. A surprising number of plants did survive, evolving highly successful techniques for moisture conservation, survival on poor soils, and defences against bushfires. It is these adaptations that give Australian trees their distinctive characteristics.

The majority of Australian plant families have members with relatively small, rigid or hard leaves. These plants are known as sclerophyllous and their leaves demonstrate highly successful adaptations to arid conditions and poor soil.

Many trees and shrubs, notably the eucalypts, developed layers of hard cells beneath the leaf surface. This enabled the leaves to remain rigid during droughts instead of suffering tissue collapse like many other species. Some of the acacias modified their leaves into long, narrow shapes to cut down the absorption of radiation, and the casuarinas, for example the desert oak, dispensed with leaves altogether; they appear as tiny circlets of scales along the stems.

Other adaptations include the thick corky bark of many trees that insulates the sap from sun and bushfires; long numerous roots that seek out the tiniest drop of moisture and hard, woody seeds that can survive until conditions are right for germination.

Fire in the Australian bush.

Many of these dry-adapted plants can survive on inadequate nutrients and minerals, and flourish on poor soils. Australian soils are extremely ancient and the comparative lack of recent volcanic activity has meant a dearth of new soil production. Long periods of weathering and leaching have starved the soils of nutrients, producing conditions that favour hard-leaved (sclerophyllous) vegetation.

Fire has long been a dominant feature in sclerophyll forest and the plants have evolved many adaptations to survive. The eucalypts often have highly heat resistant bark which protects the epicormic buds underneath. These buds remain dormant until fire destroys the tree's canopy then they burst into life, sprouting new branches. Other plants, such as banksias, hakeas and casuarinas, produce large quantities of seeds which are protected in the soil or in woody fruits and which germinate after fire. Wattles, although readily destroyed by fire, produce large quantities of hard seeds which are cracked open by the heat of the fire, enabling water to be absorbed and germination to take place.

There are therefore three major elements in Australia's flora: the relict Gondwanaland flora, typified by the southern beeches of Tasmania; the Asian element seen in the northern parts of the continent, resulting from links with Asia; and the more recent 'Australian'-type flora which has seen the unique development of many endemic plants, well-adapted to our climate, soils and recurrent bushfires.

Australia's climate varies markedly from the arid centre to the moist east coast; and from the tropical north to the temperate south. This climatic variation, combined with topography and soil types, has produced several distinctive habitats.

The largest single habitat, the great central desert and semi-desert zone, supports very few trees. Bordering this region in the south is a belt of vegetation called mallee, consisting of dwarfed eucalypt trees. The central grassy deserts are fringed with woodland, open country with scattered shrubs and trees. In some areas of tropical Australia woodland extends from the interior right to the coast.

However, as the coast is neared around much of the continent the woodland gives way to forests. Densest of these forests is the rainforest where tree canopies intermingle to form a closed roof. Rainforest occurs in a narrow broken belt east of the Great Divide and has its most complex development in northern Queensland. Less dense are the stately wet forests of mountain ash and similar hardwood trees which occur mainly in the south-east, including Tasmania, and in the isolated karri forests of south-western Australia.

Most common is the dry forest, a habitat that typifies Australian vegetation and is found over much of the continent. It is fairly open forest, dominated by the form, nature and living habits of the eucalypts.

The following are some of the more notable trees found in Australia.

Acacia

There are over 800 species of acacia recognised in Australia. As such they are one of the major components of the Australian bush. They vary in stature from low prostrate shrubs to tall trees, and because of their adaptive qualities are found in most ecosystems, being particularly at home in the dry forest with the eucalypts. Wattles are the best known acacias. The Australian golden wattle has even been officially proclaimed the national floral emblem.

Wattles were so-called because the long flexible twigs of some species were used by the early settlers to construct hut walls in the traditional European method of reinforced mud, called wattle and daub.

The flowering wattles are the most numerous and familiar members of the genus, being well-represented in each State. Their glowing masses of golden blossom are as familiar a feature of the Australian landscape as the eucalypts. The fluffy balls and spikes of their blooms range in colour from gold to off-white. The puff-ball effect of the flowers comes from the numerous stamens on each of the tiny flowers which cluster tightly into a ball. Each flower comprises minute petals rising from a cup—up to one hundred flowers make each single golden ball.

Some acacias, however, have quite inconspicuous flowers, one such being the mulga. It is found in a great belt stretching across the centre of the continent. Mulga grows up to 10 metres high and is extremely drought resistant. The wood of the trunk is dense and brownish red, surrounded by thick white sapwood. Myall is another acacia found in the semi-arid interior. It is a small highly drought resistant tree growing to about 8 metres. It flowers only after heavy rains when small, nectarless dark yellow flowers appear.

Another species of acacia is the weeping myall or boree, a slender graceful tree of about 12 metres high. Its wood is the hardest and heaviest of all the acacias.

Gidgees of various species are acacias with a form similar to mulga. They grow to about 8 metres with a moderately dense crown of pale green foliage.

Acacia leaves are varied. Most species do not have leaves at all, merely phyllodes or stalks which are flattened into leaf-like shapes, or, in some cases, adapted to a needle shape or even a spine. This adaptation is a product of a dry environment; by exposing a smaller surface to the sun and wind, moisture loss is reduced.

All acacias are legumes or pod-bearers, with flat seed cases. The pods are often decorative—coiled, looped and twisted—and the seeds have a very hard outer covering

Mallee growth in the Little Desert of Victoria.

A typical Australian bush scene. *Eucalyptus* species with a sclerophyllous understorey that includes *Acacia* species and some members of the Cyperaceae family.

which needs heat to crack it before the seeds can germinate. The seed may remain dormant for years. But where a bushfire is followed by rain, water will enter the cracked seed pod and start the germination process—wattles are often the first trees to spring up after bushfires and they are very fast growing. Few wattle species, however, grow into large trees or live very long.

A unique wattle is the brigalow, *Acacia harpophylla*, which dominates a great belt averaging 240 kilometres wide and stretching 1440 kilometres south from the latitude of Mackay to the New South Wales border. This acacia has a narrow rough-barked trunk and tangled foliage. The trees grow close together, the average height of the canopy being between 9 and 15 metres.

Adansonia
Baobabs

The baobab, a native of dry outback areas, is one of the most unusual trees in Australia. The tree has a huge, squat, bottle-shaped trunk often more than 20 metres in diameter but only 10 metres in height, and a low crown of twisted branches. For about five months the tree carries leaves, then they fall off during the dry season. The huge trunk provides the tree with internal storage of food and water during the long periods of drought. The wood is light and fleshy, consisting mostly of hollow bark-covered chambers which store water—some baobabs have yielded as much as 360 litres of fresh water. The baobab has white waxy flowers and large seed pods containing seeds set in a mass of bread-like pulp. Derived from the African baobabs, with no close relatives in this country, it is one of Australia's few native deciduous trees.

Angophora
Apple gums

This genus is sometimes described as a sub-division of the eucalypts. *Angophora* species are almost indistinguishable from true eucalypts but their flowers do not have caps and the fruits are less woody and more papery. They are native to the rugged, fast-draining sandstone country of the east, from north-eastern Queensland down to eastern Victoria. They are handsome trees with orange or pinkish bark which peels unevenly from the trunk. The juvenile foliage comprises pale green heart-shaped leaves and the mature leaves are drooping and up to 12.5 centimetres long. The masses of cream flowers are followed by ribbed gumnut-like fruits.

Included in this genus are the rough-barked apple, smooth-barked apple, narrow-leaved apple, broad-leaved apple and dwarf apple. The name *Angophora* is from the Greek words *aggos* and *phero* and means cup-bearer, an allusion to the fruits.

Araucaria
Native pines

The hoop and bunya pines are the only species of this small genus that occur naturally on mainland Australia, although the Norfolk Island pine is widely planted along Australian beaches. The hoop and bunya are outstanding conifers, tall and straight with a symmetrical outline. The branches are arranged in a domed or layered crown or in tiers and the trunk is almost perfectly cylindrical, covered with dark, rough bark often fissured or ridged with horizontal rings.

The hoop pine is considered the most valuable of Australia's limited range of native softwoods and has been of considerable economic importance in Queensland. The timber of the hoop pine is softer than the bunya. The hoop pine has seeds as large as a small hen's egg that are filled with highly nutritious nut-like 'meat' which when roasted tastes like chestnut. Both these pines are inhabitants of Queensland's rainforests.

The Norfolk Island pine (*Araucaria heterophylla*), although not occurring naturally on mainland Australia, is widely planted along beach fronts.

Banksia

A familiar sight in the Australian bush, banksias were named after the famous botanist Sir Joseph Banks. They were reputedly the first plant collected at what is now Botany Bay. Members of the ancient Proteaceae family, there are 71 species of banksia altogether—57 are found in the south-west of the continent and the remaining 14 are spread along the eastern and southern coasts and tablelands. Although most of the species are classified as shrubs there are several that reach tree size.

All banksia species have certain features in common, including the form of their flowers. The individual flowers have no stalk and are very narrow. They are carried in dense spikes containing more than a thousand flowers that are embedded in crowded rows around a thick woody axis. These spikes eventually become large fruiting cones, on which the withered flowers remain for a long time as dry bristly fuzz. The magnificent flower spikes vary from bluish green to yellow to red. They flower at all times of the year, in every habitat from the spray-lashed islands of Bass Strait to the tropics and high slopes of the Alps.

Brachychiton
Kurrajongs and lacebarks

There are about twelve species of this genus, all endemic to Australia, including the Illawarra flame tree, the lacebark tree, the bottle tree, and the kurrajong. They are most variable trees, in size, trunk shape and leaves; the flowers are generally bell-shaped. Those native to the semi-tropical forests of the moist east coast grow tall and flower profusely on the bare tree after the leaves have fallen. Others, native to the arid regions, are smaller in size with bloated water-storing trunks. Their flowers are not as spectacular and tend to appear under the new summer foliage.

Callitris
Cypress pines

These are the most commonly seen conifers in Australia and are found in all States. There are about sixteen species including the black cypress, white cypress and Port Jackson pine. The trees are generally of tall formal cypress shape with extremely fine foliage. The leaves of mature specimens have adapted into tiny scales; the foliage on seedlings is short and needle-like. The bark is usually dark and the hard, dense timber is pale and colourfully knot-marked; it is often used for flooring. A useful feature of the wood is its resistance to white ants. The cypresses grow between 10 and 20 metres in height, some species being drought resistant and growing well on the rocky ridges and slopes of the arid woodlands in central Australia.

Cassia
Sennas or shower trees

Australia has about thirty species of endemic cassias which vary in form from low spreading shrubs to fairly large tropical trees. All have attractive pinnate leaves with a variable number of small leaflets appearing alternately down the leaf stalk. The brilliant yellow flowers are five-petalled and open, with prominent stamens. Some of the flowers are perfumed and they all cross-pollinate, producing beautiful hybrids. Various species have flowers appearing in long, weeping sprays while others appear in rigid spikes at the end of branchlets. They are often long-flowering, and the flowers are followed by long, pea-like pods which can be up to 60 centimetres long in some species. The name *Cassia* is from the Hebrew name for one of the species, *quetsi'oth*.

Casuarina and Allocasuarina
She-oaks

The well-known genus *Casuarina* was split into three genera in 1982. Most of the Australian species have been placed in *Allocasuarina* but five (*C. cristata, C. cunninghamiana, C. equisetifolia, C. glauca* and *C. obesa*) remain as *Casuarina*. The third genus, *Gymnostoma*, contains a single species not found in Australia.

She-oaks or casuarinas range in size from small shrubs to tall trees up to 30 metres in height, one of the tallest species being the river oak which grows along coastal and inland watercourses. Its deep root network holds the sand in which it grows, creating a natural defence for river banks against floods and erosion.

The desert oak, which can often be seen in fairly large stands on the red dunes of sand-ridge country, also has very deep roots to seek moisture from the sands. It has thick, corky bark and vertical needle-like foliage to reduce water loss. The desert oak grows to 20 metres, a height unmatched by any other tree in comparable conditions anywhere in the world.

The coast she-oak is widely distributed around Australia's coastline and ranges from a low, gnarled form to an erect tree of about 15 metres.

The genus was called *Casuarina* because of the likeness of the drooping foliage to the feathers of the cassowary bird. The common name of she-oak is said to be derived from the inferior oak-like timber. The wood of *Casuarina* is hard, dense and straight-grained and was much used by the early settlers.

All casuarinas have drooping foliage that consists of branchlets, not the needle-like leaves they appear to be. The true leaves are tiny scales forming a circlet at the branchlet joints. The reduction of the leaves, along with the thick corky bark, are adaptations to a hot and arid climate. Tiny, reddish flowers are carried on the ends of the branchlets. The seeds grow inside a woody cone on the female tree and when they are ripe the cone opens and the seeds, which have tiny wings, are wafted away on the wind. The genus is chiefly Australian although some species grow through tropical Asia from east Africa to the South Pacific islands.

Elaeocarpus
Blueberry ashes

This large genus of tropical and sub-tropical rainforest trees has about twenty species endemic to Australia, including ebony heart, silver quandong, and the blueberry ash. Many are valuable timber trees. The attractive bell-shaped fragrant flowers are borne in small sprays and are white, pink or cream. The flowers are followed by a crop of brilliant blue or green fruits. They are slender graceful trees with slightly toothed laurel-like leaves.

Eucalyptus

Eucalypts are a uniquely Australian genus of trees. Although most dominant in dry forest, they have adapted to a wide range of conditions and occupy both dry and wet sites, flourishing in all topographical conditions.

William Dampier, landing in north-western Australia in 1688, was the first to describe trees exuding what he perceived as gum. In fact, the substance exuded is kino, not gum, but the common name 'gum tree' has remained with the species.

The genus was named *Eucalyptus* from the Greek words *eu*, well, and *kalyptos*, covered, a name chosen because the flower buds of all species are covered by a tight-fitting cap. The genus includes about 550 species, which, for general purposes, can be divided into six groups according to their bark.

The best known and largest group is commonly referred to as the gums. These have smooth bark and are called gum because the first species seen to yield a large quantity of kino all had smooth bark. These include the blue gum, red gum, grey gum, rose gum, ghost gum and salmon gum, so-called for the colour of their timber or bark. The bark is shed annually in strips starting from the top of the trunk.

Eucalypts are quick to produce new growth after bushfires.

Gum tree bark is usually shed annually in strips starting from the top of the trunk.

Stringybarks have long fibres of soft, thick, fibrous bark which extends right up the tree into the branches and comes away in strips.

Peppermints, which contain aromatic oil in their leaves, also have fibrous bark.

The bloodwoods, with soft, flaky-fibrous bark, exude a greater amount of kino than the other eucalypts, the dark red drips having the appearance of bloodstains.

The ironbarks have the thickest, hardest and heaviest bark of all. It is dark grey, furrowed and impregnated with kino, so strong that it is difficult to penetrate with a knife. These trees can grow in very poor soils and withstand drought and fire.

The box group of eucalypts, so-called because their timber resembled that of the European box tree, has thin scaly or flaky bark very firmly attached to the lower trunk.

There are several other eucalypts which do not fall into the above categories. The scribbly gums, related to the mountain ashes, have smooth bark decorated with squiggly heiroglyphics caused by boring moth larvae. The blackbutt has peppermint-like bark in the lower trunk and gum bark on the upper regions. The spotted gum, although a bloodwood, has gum bark and the tallow-wood has shiny, greasy, yellow-brown timber.

12

Eucalypts are quickly able to produce new leafy shoots when damaged by fire, pests or storms. This is done by means of naked buds—a small bud on a thin stem protruding from the growing tip of each leaf. This bud has the potential to develop into a new shoot, but normally all the naked buds do not develop in this manner. Only those at the tips of the main branches produce new shoots, those lower down are kept dormant by hormones in the tree. Should the higher growing tips be damaged, the hormonal check is released and the lower buds start growing, assuming the role of leading shoots. In this manner, the eucalypts can produce several generations of new branching in several weeks.

Eucalypt leaves vary widely according to species in both width and length, ranging from spear-shaped to heart-shaped. The flowers of all eucalypt species have a cup-shaped lid or operculum which covers each flower bud, popping off and dropping as the dense mass of stamens expand for the colourful seasonal display.

Eucalypts yield several valuable oils and because of their enormous quantity of flowers, are an important honey source. The timber of many species, such as jarrah and blackbutt, provides some of the best hardwoods in the world. Eucalypts have also become an important export, used for reforestation in many of the world's most barren areas.

This large family also occupies a wide variety of forms, from the exceptionally hardy snow gum which can withstand conditions above 1500 metres in the Australian Alps, to the river red gums and ghost gums which survive the arid deserts and dried up water-courses of the harsh centre of the continent.

Eucalypts of the dry forest, because of the poorer soils, seldom grow higher than 35 metres. These eucalypts include the stringybarks, spotted gum, red bloodwood, marri and jarrah, a valuable hardwood which is found only in Western Australia.

On the rich loam soils of the high rainfall areas of the wet forest, eucalypts such as the messmate, alpine ash, Sydney blue gum, blackbutt, tallow-wood and karri reach their greatest size. The tallest species of all is the Victorian and Tasmanian mountain ash, one specimen in Tasmania, at 98.15 metres high, has been recorded as the world's tallest hardwood tree. The straight trunks of the mountain ash, apart from rough bark at the base, are clean and smooth, sometimes hung with ribbons of dead bark which the tree sheds as it grows in girth. In south-western Australia there is a unique wet forest of giant eucalypts known as karri which loom out of the understorey, rising without a branch to a leafy crown.

Woodland eucalypts are generally less than 25 metres high and have short squat trunks with spreading crowns of heavy branches. Western woodland species include salmon gum, tuart and wandoo; eastern and northern species include red gum, ironbark and box tree groups. The salmon gum is one of the most beautiful of all the gums. The bark is continually shed from trunk and

The Valley of the Giants—a forest of huge karri and tingle trees near Nornalup in the south-west corner of Western Australia.

13

branches exposing a smooth salmon pink surface, sometimes with grey patches.

A dry inland region of the country, extending from the south-west corner of New South Wales through Victoria into South Australia and Western Australia, is home to the mallee form of eucalypt. This form occurs when the tree, instead of growing a single trunk with a number of roots in the normal manner, produces several smaller stems, all of about the same thickness and height, from a single, greatly thickened root stock. This results in a cluster of bare stems diverging somewhat from the base, supporting an umbrella-shaped crown of foliage. These low, close-growing trees create a sea of virtually unbroken vegetation stretching for hundreds of kilometres. About twenty species of eucalypt are found only as mallee, but given poor soil, low rainfall and a prevalence of fire, many other eucalypts will adopt the mallee form.

Desert conditions do not encourage the growth of large trees, but one eucalypt, the ghost gum, is a typical central Australian tree. Usually occurring in a solitary state, the ghost gum can grow to 20 metres and has an attractively gnarled trunk and branches. Its smooth white bark re-flects radiation efficiently, keeping down the internal trunk temperature. It carries masses of creamy flowers followed by small cup-shaped gumnuts.

At the other extreme is the snow gum, the only plant of mainland Australia that has been able to establish itself thoroughly above the snowline. At lower altitudes, between 1000 and 1800 metres, the snow gum forms dense woodlands of low-branching trees. It can also grow at altitudes a little above 1800 metres, but here it is found in a stunted, wind-blasted form.

About the only habitat that the eucalypts are not found in is the rainforest. The dark humid interiors and damp leaf-littered floors of this environment are not conducive to this group of trees.

A small ghost gum has made a precarious home in a rock crevice in a canyon in the George Hill Range in central Australia.

A magnificent old river red gum with partly eroded roots stretches across Mt Emu Creek in Victoria.

Ficus
Figs

Although the species of figs that produce the most succulent fruits have been introduced into Australia from the Middle East, there are about fifty species of figs which are native to this continent. Most of them are found in the rainforest, although they are generally quite adaptable. The Moreton Bay fig, a large spreading tree to 40 metres, is found in parks and gardens throughout Australia.

A number of the rainforest figs start their lives as epiphytes (plants which perch on or adhere to other plants but obtain nutrients and water from the environment, not their host). When their roots reach the ground they envelop their host tree, finally killing it. These are known as strangler figs. They survive as one of the largest trees of the rainforest, the decaying stems of their hosts sometimes visible within the deep folds of their gnarled trunks.

The strangler fig's roots, growing vertically downwards around the trunk of its host tree, form a curtain, thus the trees are often referred to as curtain figs.

Flindersia
Australian ashes

This genus includes teak, Queensland maple, leopardwood and cudgerie, mostly inhabitants of the cool moist Australian coastal forests. An exception is leopardwood which prefers the arid outback of New South Wales and Queensland and reaches a height of 15 metres. It gains its name from the mottled pattern of charcoal grey and cream on the trunk. The rainforest species are tall straight trees often more than 30 metres high. All usually have dark glossy green foliage with large leaflets. Flowers are small and insignificant but the fruits are often interesting.

Grevillea

There are over 200 species of *Grevillea*, many of them trees. The best-known is the silky oak, so-called because of the resemblance of its timber to the English oak. This tree can reach a height of more than 30 metres and is often seen in sub-tropical rainforest. It has an upright habit with slightly upward-pointing branches decked with silver-backed fern-like leaves. Its brilliant orange-yellow flowers turn the tree into a blazing pyramid of colour. Beefwood, another member of the *Grevillea* genus, is a rough-barked tree up to 10 metres high. It is found in arid areas along watercourses or on floodplains.

Grevillea were named for Charles Greville, a friend of Sir Joseph Banks and founder of England's Royal Horticultural Society.

Melaleuca
Paperbarks

Paperbarks belong to the genus *Melaleuca* from the Greek words *melos*, black, and *leukos*, white, referring to the mottled black and white bark on some species. There are about 140 species, known mostly for their decorative peeling bark and colourful flower spikes on which hundreds of long-stamened flowers are arranged in the form of a bottlebrush, generally white or cream in the tree-sized species. They range in size from small shrubs to large trees up to 30 metres high. The most common species is the broad-leaved paperbark which grows in the coastal brackish swamps of eastern Australia.

The handsome paperbarks grow to about 12 metres and have very soft papery bark made up of many thin sheets which peel off and hang in tatters. This bark comprises layers of dead cells which form outside the living bark to provide protection against water loss and extremes in temperature. As the tree grows, the dead cells, unable to grow with it, become detached in sheets. Sheets of paperbark were greatly appreciated by the Aborigines who used them as covering for their shelters and to make drinking and water-carrying utensils.

Xanthorrhoea
Grass trees

The grass tree (yacca or blackboy) is a distant relative of the lilies, found only in Australia. Archaic in form, it has long narrow leaves which cap a black, irregular trunk. A tall, thin, flowering spike sometimes protrudes from the leafy crown. This spike is covered with tens of thousands of tiny, creamy flowers. In some grass trees a new flowering spike is produced each year, yet an identical tree, close by, may not flower at all for ten to fifteen years.

The trunks are made up of the ends of thousands of thin leaf bases, tightly packed together in rings. The leaves grow outwards from a spongy fibrous core, eventually breaking off. The plant produces one complete circlet of leaves each year, making them among the slowest growing plants in the world. They are also highly resistant to insect and fire damage because of a protective jacket on the leaf bases formed by hardened resinous red or yellow gum. After a fire, the blackened stumps of grass trees rapidly produce a new mantle of leaves.

These trees, which have dotted the landscape for over 100 million years, number seventeen species which vary in size and occur in Queensland, the southern States and Western Australia, where the dry sandy soil provides ideal conditions.

Other Genera

There are many other species of trees found throughout Australia, the genera described above merely being among the best known examples of the continent's magnificent trees. Other stately specimens that can be seen in the rainforests include *Cryptocarya* species such as the brown beech, which grows to 30 metres, and the red cedar, *Toona*, a famous timber tree that is now rare because of indiscriminate logging in earlier days. This tree grows to about 40 metres with a tall straight trunk and buttresses around the base. It is deciduous, with compound leaves and small, perfumed pink flowers hanging from the branchlets in spring.

Lilly-pillies (*Syzygium* and *Acmena*) are also seen in the rainforests. Most are shapely medium-sized trees with glossy dark green leaves and a wealth of attractive flowers and vividly coloured, delicately sweet berries.

The slow-growing kauri pine *(Agathis)*, a tall straight tree to 50 metres with scaly well-marked bark, is also found in Queensland's rainforests. Here, too, are seen the *Backhousia* species, which include the aniseed tree, lemon ironwood and shatterwood. Some of these species have very showy flowers and their foliage is often strongly aromatic.

Sassafras *(Dodyphora* and *Athosperma)* and the ancient southern beeches *(Nothofagus)* are both found in cool temperate rainforest. Sassafras has dark green glossy leaves and fragrant bark and leaves. The Tasmanian and Victorian species of *Nothofagus, N. cunninghamii,* grows up to 50 metres with a trunk up to 2 metres in diameter. The niggerhead beech *(N. moorei)* is found in New South Wales and Queensland.

Tulipwood *(Harpullia)* is an inhabitant of Australia's warm eastern coastal forest and has striking glossy pinnate leaves with three to six elliptical leaflets. These trees are valued for their magnificent timber which is streaked with dark brown and yellow.

There are about nine species of *Pittosporum* in Australia and they occur in both rainforest and desert environments. They are handsome evergreens with fragrant flowers and seed capsules which hold the seeds embedded in a mass of sticky resin. The Queensland pittosporum and the Victorian box or native daphne are fine examples of this genus.

The pencil and King Billy pines *(Athrotaxis)* and the Huon pine *(Dacrydium)* are all endemic Tasmanian plants. They are slow-growing trees that thrive in the mountain forests.

One of the most beautiful trees in the world is endemic to Western Australia. It is the Western Australian Christmas tree *(Nuytsia)* which has glorious, profuse, golden yellow flowers. It is a root parasite, obtaining its nourishment through the roots of nearby host trees.

The majority of this country's distinctive *Hakea* and *Hibiscus* are classed as shrubs but there are several of tree size. Several hakeas occur as trees, most of them with conspicuous flowers. All have nut-like woody fruits which split in half to release two winged seeds. The pin-cushion hakea, which can reach small tree proportions, has eye-catching small red flowers packed in dense 5 centimetre globular heads. Each flower unrolls a single creamy yellow filament to give a pin-cushion effect.

The cottonwood, a member of the *Hibiscus* genus, is another striking small tree often found in swampy brackish saltwater inlets. It has profuse bright yellow flowers during the summer.

Fog among the tree ferns and mountain ash in the Otways in Victoria.

Acacia aneura
Mulga

This small tree is native to the arid interior of all mainland States and is especially abundant on the Western Plains of New South Wales. The phyllodes are narrow and greyish and the flowers are rod-like and bright yellow, occurring in spring or other times, depending on rain.

Mulga has many uses: the foliage is used for livestock fodder, the wood for fencing and carved ornaments.

Acacia baileyana
Cootamundra wattle

The most widespread and popular of the wattles, this small tree grows to 10 metres high by 6 metres across. It has bluish grey foliage and profuse, gold, ball-shaped flowers which occur late in winter. Pods are bluish when young. The wattle originally occurred naturally in the Cootamundra district, but is now widely cultivated and naturalised in many areas.

Acacia elata
Cedar wattle
This handsome tree grows to 30 metres with a distinct trunk and narrow-domed crown. Leaves are dark green and pale yellow, ball-shaped flowers appear in summer. Distribution is mostly in gullies and on the banks of east-flowing streams in New South Wales, southern Queensland and eastern Victoria.

Acacia implexa
Hickory wattle
This summer-flowering *Acacia* is a small to medium-sized tree, growing to 12 metres high. It bears cream ball-shaped flowers and has light-green, sickle-shaped phyllodes. Hickory wattle is found throughout Queensland, New South Wales, the Australian Capital Territory and Victoria.

19

Acacia mearnsii
Black wattle
A slender tree, the black wattle grows between 8 and 16 metres tall with an erect trunk and narrow-domed crown, becoming broader when grown in the open. Cream, ball-shaped flowers occur in spring. This Acacia is found mostly in open forests in New South Wales, Victoria and Tasmania.

Acacia pycnantha
Australian golden wattle
This wattle is the Australian floral emblem. It is a small tree, to about 10 metres high, with large brilliantly gold ball-shaped flowers occurring in spring. It is found throughout New South Wales, Victoria and South Australia and naturalised in other States.

Acmena smithii
(Syn. *Eugenia smithii*)
Lilly-pilly
A medium-sized tree growing to 20 metres, the lilly-pilly is usually found on the margins of coastal streams or in deep protected gullies. Mature specimens take on a slightly buttressed form. White fluffy flowers are borne in summer, followed by pretty pink fleshy berries that are edible raw and make a tasty jam. Distribution is throughout Queensland, New South Wales, Victoria and the Northern Territory. *Acmena* is a Greek word meaning 'buxom, beautiful, or in youthful prime', referring to the flowers and fruit.

Adansonia gregorii
Baobab
Found across the northern areas of Western Australia and the Northern Territory, this remarkable tree grows to 14 metres and develops a huge, swollen bottle-like trunk on ageing. It can reach 20 metres in diameter and has a shallow crown of twisted branches. Large baobabs often develop hollows inside their bulbous trunks; police sometimes kept a prisoner securely inside the tree hollow for the night while travelling through the bush with a suspect.

Agathis robusta
Kauri pine

This evergreen, coniferous species comes from the rain-forests of Queensland and will grow to 50 metres. The leaves are dark green and glossy and the bark is scaly and well marked. It bears 12 centimetre long ovoid female cones.

Allocasuarina decaisneana
(Syn. *Casuarina distyla*)
Desert oak

A medium-sized (up to 15 metres) she-oak, this species grows in the very arid areas of South Australia and the Northern Territory. It has soft, needle-like foliage and bears large ovoid fruit. In older days the iron-hard timber was used for war clubs, boomerangs and carpenter's tools.

Allocasuarina verticillata
(Syn. *Casuarina stricta*)
Drooping she-oak
Long and pendulous branchlets give this tree a most attractive appearance. Distributed throughout New South Wales, the Australian Capital Territory, Victoria, South Australia and Tasmania, this small rounded she-oak grows to 10 metres, often less.

Angophora costata
Smooth-barked apple
An evergreen, this species grows to 30 metres high and has pitted, salmon-pink bark. Branches are often gnarled and twisted and whitish cream flowers occur in spring and early summer. The bark is often stained red from freely exuded kino.

Araucaria bidwillii
Bunya pine
Rough, almost black, bark characterises this native of Queensland. It is a tall, straight tree, growing to 40 metres with symmetrically arranged branches. Leaves are lanceolate and sharply pointed and it bears very large cones with edible seeds.

Araucaria cunninghamiana
Hoop pine
Found in Queensland, New South Wales and Papua New Guinea, the hoop pine grows to 40 metres high. Its leaves are narrow, pointed, crowded and curved inwards and the cones are about 8 centimetres long.

Backhousia anisata

Aniseed tree

This shapely evergreen tree has strongly aniseed-scented leaves. White flowers with prominent anthers occur in summer. The tree grows to 25 metres high in its native habitat, but it is much smaller in cultivation. It is found along the coastal watercourses and forests around the Bellinger, Hastings and Camden Haven rivers in New South Wales.

Backhousia myrtifolia

Grey myrtle

Distributed throughout the rainforest and coastal gullies of Queensland and New South Wales, this small tree grows to 7 metres high with an open habit. It bears white flowers in summer with large greenish sepals. Other members of this genus often have strongly aromatic foliage.

Banksia marginata
Silver banksia
This banksia varies in stature according to its environment, from dwarf and shrubby where winds are harsh, to erect and up to 10 metres high in more sheltered places. It is found throughout south-eastern Australia. Leaves are silver on the underside and yellow cylindrical flower spikes appear in spring and summer.

Banksia prionotes
Acorn banksia
This beautiful banksia is found on sandy heathlands close to the sea on the south-western coast of Western Australia. It grows to 8 metres with narrow saw-toothed leaves and 18 centimetre long cylindrical orange flower spikes that appear in winter.

26

Brachychiton acerifolius
Illawarra flame tree

Profuse red bell-shaped flowers adorn this tree in summer when the leaves are absent. An erect tree to 30 metres tall (less in cultivation), it has large light-green leaves and a conical crown. The fruit are hard, boat-shaped follicles with hairy yellow seeds enclosed in a brittle papery coat. Distribution is throughout Queensland and New South Wales.

Brachychiton discolor
Lacebark tree

Discolor is from the Greek, 'of two colours', referring to the upper (dark green) and lower (silvery) leaf surfaces of this tree. Pink flowers occur in summer when the leaves are absent, and the fruit are boat-shaped follicles. It is a handsome spreading tree to 30 metres and has an erect trunk and conical crown. It can be found throughout the forests of the eastern Australian coast from the Manning River to northern Queensland.

Brachychiton populneus
Kurrajong
A shapely evergreen tree to 10–20 metres tall and 6–8 metres wide, the kurrajong is common in the eastern States, particularly the western slopes and plains of New South Wales and Queensland. It has a stout single trunk and densely leafed medium-domed crown. Bell-shaped cream and red flowers appear in summer, followed by boat-shaped seed pods.

Brachychiton rupestre
Bottle tree
Native to Queensland, these oddly shaped trees grow to 20 metres high, with swollen bottle-like trunks. They bear small, unspectacular creamy yellow flowers from November to January.

Callistemon salignus
White bottlebrush
This bottlebrush is mainly found on alluvial soils near permanent water in Queensland and New South Wales. It has a dense habit, papery bark and narrow leaves, and usually grows to 9 metres high. Young growth is pink, and cream cylindrical flower spikes decorate the tree in summer.

Callistemon viminalis
Weeping bottlebrush
Attractive drooping branches and bright red flowers identify this spring-flowering bottlebrush. Found in central New South Wales and southern Queensland, it prefers moist soils near permanent water. When grown in the open it reaches 10 metres but can be taller in its native habitat.

Callitris preissii
Rottnest Island pine
More open and less formal than other *Callitris* species, this small tree (to 20 metres) accepts very dry conditions and is widespread over much of Queensland, New South Wales, Victoria, South Australia and Western Australia. *Callitris* species generally have foliage almost to the ground and small, scale-like leaves.

Dacrydium franklinii
Huon pine
Native to Tasmania, this tall, slow-growing conifer reaches 30 metres in height and has small leaves closely pressed to stems, and very small cones.

▶

Dryandra formosa
Showy dryandra
A large shrub or small tree, this stunning dryandra grows to 4 metres high by 2 metres in diameter and is found in Western Australia. Orange flowerheads appear in winter and leaves are narrow and closely toothed.

Erythrina variegata
Coral tree
Large and rugged looking, the coral tree grows to about 18 metres. Its brilliant showy flowers occur after leaf fall. These trees are native to the warmer regions of the country, particularly along the eastern coast.

Eucalyptus calophylla
Marri
A bloodwood tree to 10–20 metres tall, marri is found in ▶ higher rainfall areas in south-west Western Australia. It bears large clusters of cream, pink or red flowers in summer and autumn and large urn-shaped fruits. Typical of the bloodwood family, it has rough, flaky-fibrous grey bark that continues into the upper branches.

(Overleaf)
Eucalyptus camaldulensis
River red gum
Symbol of inland Australia, this large spreading tree is found along watercourses and river banks throughout the arid and semi-arid parts of the continent. It is the most widespread of all Australia's eucalypts. The bark is generally smooth, the trunk very thick, often buttressed by the large roots, with some patches of scaly bark at the base. The upper trunk and branches are smooth, blue-grey, creamy yellow or pinkish.

Eucalyptus citriodora
Lemon-scented gum

A native of Queensland, this tall graceful tree grows to at least 40 metres. It has smooth bark with a clean straight trunk and delicate tracery of slender twigs and pendulous leaves which are strongly lemon-scented. Creamy white flowers appear during mid to late winter.

Eucalyptus cladocalyx
Sugar gum ▼

The small, spreading sugar gum has been extensively planted in South Australia for stock shelter and farm timber supplies. It has pale bark and creamy white flowers which appear from early December to late February.

Eucalyptus diversicolor
Karri ▶

This majestic tree rivals the mountain ash of Tasmania as the world's tallest hardwood. Karri grows only where rainfall exceeds 1000 millimetres a year—a narrow belt of about 202 300 hectares in south-western Australia. A very large tree, growing to 70 metres, the karri has smooth bark, greyish in colour. At certain times, all the trees in a karri forest shed their bark in great tatters, exposing their gleaming new bark. The tallest fire lookout tree in the world is situated in the karri forest near Pemberton in south-west Western Australia. The tower is 61 metres above the ground.

Eucalyptus eremophila
Tall sand mallee
Attractive and profuse, the pendent flowers of the tall sand mallee are greenish yellow with a longer finger-like operculum (bud cap). It is a spring-flowering tree, growing to 10 metres and native to Western Australia.

Eucalyptus erythrocorys
Illyarie
Vibrant yellow flowers and bright red grooved operculums make the illyarie one of the most colourful of the eucalypts. This very showy tree grows to 9 metres and is found in Western Australia.

Eucalyptus erythronema
White mallee
This small, smooth-barked tree has rosy crimson flowers with golden yellow anthers which appear from September to mid-summer. The trunk and lower branches have smooth whitish grey bark; the upper twigs are pink or reddish. A native of south-west Western Australia, it is widespread in the central wheatbelt.

Eucalyptus ficifolia
Red-flowering gum
One of the most spectacular of all eucalypts, this tree is native to a very restricted locality on the south coast of Western Australia but has been extensively cultivated in other areas. Its flowers are always profuse and vary in colour from white to pink, red and orange. A small, often twisted tree, it grows to 9 metres and has rough bark and large, urn-shaped fruits. The hard woody seed pods are green at first, ripening to dark grey-brown and remain on the tree for several years.

39

Eucalyptus forrestiana
Fuchsia gum
This very ornamental eucalypt grows to about 7 metres and has smooth grey bark which is shed in long strips. The species has distinctive pendulous, large, red, bell-like, four-angled buds and fruit which are bright red at first, turning brown with time. It flowers intermittently from early October to early autumn, and is native to south-west Western Australia, near Esperance.

Eucalyptus grandis
Flooded gum
A wet forest tree found in Queensland and northern New South Wales, this species is known as flooded gum as it grows well in gullies and valleys subjected to flooding. A most imposing tree, its tall smooth trunk, up to 45 metres, often pure white, rises sheer from the tangled understorey of palms, wattles and other shrubs.

40

Eucalyptus leucoxylon
Yellow gum
Flowers of this medium-sized tree vary in colour from white to pink or red. It is a woodland species, found in New South Wales, Victoria and South Australia. It has a smooth bark, straight trunk and shapely crown.

Eucalyptus megacornuta
Warty yate
The warty bud caps or operculums of this slender tree are between 3 and 4 centimetres long. Found in Western Australia, the warty yate grows between 7 and 12 metres high and has a profusion of yellow-green flowers in winter and spring.

41

◄ *Eucalyptus melliodora*
Yellow box

Usually seen as an open-savannah species, yellow box is found in Queensland, New South Wales, the Australian Capital Territory and Victoria. It is a handsome medium-sized to tall spreading tree which grows to 30 metres. The sturdy straight trunk is covered with finely fissured, slightly fibrous, bark.

Eucalyptus obliqua
Messmate

One of the taller eucalypts, messmate can reach 60 metres. It is found on the rich loam soils of wet forest areas in Queensland, New South Wales, Victoria, Tasmania and South Australia.

Eucalyptus papuana sens lat
Ghost gum

The white-boled ghost gums of the interior are familiar to many in the paintings of Aboriginal artist, Albert Namatjira. This eucalypt has quite an extensive range from Western Australia to across the Northern Territory and into Queensland. It also occurs in Papua New Guinea. It is an upright tree, growing to 16 metres, with pendulous leaves and branches and smooth white bark. In Central Australia it occurs as a solitary tree, often with no other tree in sight. On rocky cliff faces in broken country the tree is stunted and gnarled with twisted and tortuous trunk and branches.

◀ *Eucalyptus pauciflora*
Snow gum
The outstanding plant of the Australian Alps, this species has a smooth white attractively blotched bark. It is the only tree in mainland Australia that has been able to establish itself thoroughly above the snowline. Occurring in a very wide range of altitudes and climatic conditions, the species exhibits different characteristics in different locations. Between 1000 and 1800 metres it forms dense woodlands of low-branching trees and at higher altitudes it is found buried in snowdrifts, in stunted windblasted shapes. The base colour changes to pink, yellow, pale green and bronze red at various periods.

Eucalyptus regnans
Mountain ash
This majestic tree, the world's tallest and most magnificent hardwood, grows to 90 metres. It is found in regions of high rainfall and on deep soils in central Victoria and the north-eastern corner of Tasmania. The straight trunks have rough bark at the base but are clean and smooth for the rest of their length. The crown is open and somewhat sparse.

Eucalyptus rossii
Inland scribbly gum or white gum
Found in New South Wales and the Australian Capital Territory, this species is a medium-sized tree to 15 metres with white smooth bark, often with dark grey streaks. The abstract designs decorating this species are produced by the larva of a small moth, *Ogmograptis scribula*. They form a fascinating pattern when the bark is shed from the tree. These trees often have massive swollen trunks and transversely ridged branches.

Eucalyptus salubris
Gimlet
This tree gets its name from the unusual trunk shape which resembles a gimlet or corkscrew. It is a medium-sized tree, growing to 20 metres. Distribution is throughout Western Australia.

◄ *Eucalyptus sideroxylon*
Red ironbark or mugga

The best of the ironbarks, this tree is distributed through-out Queensland, New South Wales and Victoria. It is medium-sized, growing to about 15 metres. The black, deeply furrowed bark, as in all ironbarks, is impregnated with kino which hardens on exposure to the air. The leaves are grey and flowers vary in colour from cream to pink to red, the latter being particularly attractive.

Eucalyptus torquata
Coral gum

A rough-barked, small spreading tree growing to 8 metres, this species has profuse pink flowers with grooved and beaked, coral-red operculums. The honey-perfumed flowers appear from September to February and then intermittently throughout autumn.

Eucalyptus wandoo
Wandoo

A typical tree of the open woodlands, wandoo rarely exceeds 22 metres and has a large crown with long thin branches. Its bark is shed right to ground level, and the disclosed surface is whitish yellow, with red patches. Pieces of bark sometimes remain clinging to the trunk as far up as the main branches. Wandoo wood is extremely hard, stiff and durable and both the timber and bark are a source of tannin.

►

49

Eucalyptus woodwardii
Lemon-flowered gum
Large, showy yellow flowers adorn this native eucalypt of Western Australia. An erect, slender tree, it grows to about 10 metres. Because of its handsome flowers, foliage and bark it has become a popular decorative species in inland towns.

Ficus macrophylla
Moreton Bay fig
This large spreading tree grows to about 30 metres high and spreads to about 6 metres. It is found along the east coast from Jervis Bay to Cape York Peninsula. A magnificently noble species, it has a massive, buttressed trunk, wide-spreading surface roots and a broadly rounded dense crown. It produces edible figs, about 2.5 centimetres long.

Ficus virens
White fig
The curtain fig at Yungaburra in Queensland is a good example. Here, a strangler fig has germinated on a sloping tree trunk, sending down its roots vertically so that they have formed a curtain hanging from the trunk. With a normal tree the strangler fig's roots go straight down and envelop the trunk.

Flindersia schottiana
(Syn. *F. pubescens*)
Cudgerie
The rainforests of Queensland and New South Wales are home to this large tree which can grow as tall as 40 metres. It bears small fragrant flowers and 10 centimetre long fruits. Leaflets are slightly curved.

◀ *Grevillea robusta*
Silky oak
A tall slender evergreen tree, the silky oak grows to 30 metres, developing a pyramid-like shape. It has light green leaves and bright orange-yellow toothbrush-shaped flowers that are abundant in October and November. Silky oaks are found in coastal gullies and forests from the mid–north coast of New South Wales to the Atherton Tableland, rarely more than 100 kilometres from the coast.

Hakea laurina
Pin-cushion hakea
A small evergreen tree, 4–6 metres tall, this species mostly has a single main trunk and low branches, forming a narrow domed crown. It is native to Western Australia, around the south-western coast from Perth to Esperance. The red flowers with their creamy yellow styles appear abundantly from April to July.

Melaleuca lanceolata
Moonah trees
These small trees (7 metres) are found throughout Western Australia, Victoria and South Australia. They bear creamy white flowers in loose spikes in spring and summer. These specimens, pictured on Churchill Island, Victoria, are thought to be over 500 years old.

Melaleuca linariifolia
Snow in summer or flax-leafed paperbark

Billowing masses of handsome foliage and honey-perfumed creamy white flowers make this one of the most
attractive melaleucas. It is an evergreen, 8–10 metres tall,
usually with a gnarled short main trunk and an open
medium-domed crown. The dark green leaves look especially vivid in soft, late-afternoon light.

Melaleuca quinquenervia ▼
Broad-leaved paperbark

This handsome spreading tree has attractive papery bark
and grows to 25 metres when planted on its own in damp
ground. It is often seen crowded in brackish swamps as a
collection of slim, white-trunked saplings. One of the
most reliable flowering trees in the world, it has a regular
display of cream bottlebrushes from early May to August
and also flowers at intermittent periods throughout the
year. Distribution is from Cape York to the Shoalhaven
River.

Nothofagus cunninghamii ▶
Myrtle beech

Distributed in western and north-eastern Tasmania and at
higher altitudes in southern Victoria, this slender tree
grows to 50 metres tall, mostly on a single straight trunk
with a tufted crown of small leaves, but with a broader
crown when grown in the open. Flowers and fruit are
insignificant.

◀ *Pittosporum phillyreoides*
Weeping pittosporum
The fruit of this small tree (6–8 metres tall) is an attractive small fleshy capsule which ripens to a reddish brown colour then splits to reveal dark orange-red seeds. The tree has very pendulous branches and creamy yellow flowers appear in spring and summer. It is found in the drier areas of all mainland States.

Thespesia populnea
Cotton or Indian tulip tree
Yellow, hibiscus-like flowers with a maroon centre are a feature of this small spreading tree. It grows to 15 metres and has light green heart-shaped leaves. Distribution is along the sea coasts of Queensland, and the Northern Territory.

Toona australis
Red cedar
Now rare, the red cedar was originally abundant in rain-forests right up the east coast of New South Wales and Queensland. The deep red timber is one of the world's finest furniture making timbers and as such under-went indiscriminate logging in earlier days. It grows to 40 metres with a tall straight trunk which is often buttressed.

(Previous pages and above)
Xanthorrhoea australis

Grass tree

A typical sight on the Australian landscape, fine old specimens of grass trees can be seen, with their spear-like flower spike up to 5 metres high. Veterans of many fires, their blackened stump trunks may branch once or twice to form compound heads, but more usually a single stem bears the grass-like leaves. They are found in South Australia, New South Wales, Victoria, Australian Capital Territory and Tasmania.

60

INDEX